Her Silent Song: Life in Perfect Pitch

Her Silent Song: Life in Perfect Pitch
Copyright © 2025 by Sophia Cox
All rights reserved.

All rights reserved. No part of this book may be reproduced, stored in a retrieval system, or transmitted in any form or by any means—electronic, mechanical, photocopying, recording, or otherwise—without the prior written permission of the publisher, except in the case of brief quotations used in critical articles or reviews.

ISBN: 979-8-218-66718-4

Cover design by: Kim L. Chu
Edited by: Kim L. Chu

This is a work of nonfiction. The events and experiences described in this memoir are based on the author's personal recollections. Some names and identifying details may have been changed to protect the privacy of individuals.

Printed in the United States of America
First printing edition: May 2025

For more information: Visions From Above, LLC - Sophiacox@visionsfromabove.net

Prologue

I am Here

The world hums around me. The fluorescent lights above buzz like angry bees, the floor vibrates under my feet as people rush past, their voices layering over one another like an offbeat song. Too many sounds. Too much movement. All of my senses are heightened at once.

I try to focus, to block it out, but the world doesn't quiet for me. It never does.

I want to tell them that I hear everything. That I feel everything. That my silence isn't emptiness, but fullness—a world too loud, too rich, too much to fit into words. But they don't wait. They fill the spaces where my voice should go, assuming that because I do not speak, I have nothing to say.

They are wrong.

I speak in ways they don't understand—

in the way I tap my fingers to a silent rhythm,

in the way I hum a melody only I can hear,

in the way my body sways, following the music that exists inside me even when the world is too loud.

Music is my voice. It speaks for me when words will not come.

I often laugh because I'm saying a lot even though those around me don't think so. It doesn't always seem funny—it is sad because they are not just ignoring me, it also shows they are also ignoring so many things in their own lives.

I wonder what it must be like to live in a world where silence is not mistaken for absence. Where differences are accepted and appreciated. Where people listen, not just with their ears, but with their hearts.

I wish they knew that just because my words are unspoken does not mean they are unheard.

I hope you will listen. Because if you do, you will hear me.

"Who Says" - Selena Gomez

Dedication

For my daughter, Cameron Coleman, whose voice sings beyond words.

This book is yours—your story, your truth, your silent song.

May the world listen, not just with their ears, but with their hearts.

I also dedicate this book to both my grandmother, Geneva Sturdivant and aunt, Genice Nash-Cottle. You earning your wings gave me the courage to believe in myself the way God sees me— and the way you both have raised me to know that— I am a star.

To Cam's village we appreciate and thank you for the way you show up!

With love always,
Sophia Cox

Preface

This book is the voice of my daughter Cameron, a voice the world often overlooks. As a mother and a clinical therapist, I have watched her navigate a world that struggles to understand her silence. There are times we go into a restaurant and once the waiter realizes Cameron is non-verbal the waiter won't attempt to engage my daughter any longer. There are occasions where family members and friends often respond in the same way. They have admitted they don't know how to communicate with her so they avoid it all together. Silence is not absence. Her world is rich, expressive, and filled with emotion, even if it does not come in spoken words. This book is my attempt to give her a voice and to help others listen.

I chose to write this book from her perspective because I want people to step into her world—not just as an observer, but as someone who truly listens. Too often, non-verbal individuals are spoken about but not spoken for! This book aims to change that. It is not just a story about autism, it is a story about resilience, love, and the need for deeper understanding.

While I cannot claim to know every thought she has, I have spent years learning her language—through her eyes, her expressions, her music, and her heart. This book is my interpretation of the world as I believe she experiences it, shaped by our journey together.

I hope this book challenges perceptions, opens minds, and, most importantly, teaches us all to listen—not just to words, but to the many ways people communicate. My daughter's song is silent, but it is powerful. And I invite you to listen to it with your heart.

"Can I live" Jay-Z

Table of Contents

Chapter 1: The Silence That Speaks 1

Chapter 2: The World Moves Without Me 8

Chapter 3: Invisible Walls 15

Chapter 4: A New Chapter In My Body 21

Chapter 5: Understanding Me 27

Chapter 6: Bridges and Walls 34

Chapter 7: The Weight of Expectations 40

Chapter 8: Finding Her Place 47

Chapter 9: The Language of My Heart 53

Epilogue: The Voice Within 59

Final Author's Note 61

Acknowledgements 63

About the Author 66

Reflections 67

Chapter 1:
The Silence That Speaks

They said I was perfect! The "perfect baby," as all the residents and the attending physician called me such. They came to my mother's room and requested to meet the mother who pushed out the "perfect baby" in just 3 hours with no drugs. They told my parents I had a perfect Apgar score, perfect hair, perfect head shape and the way I latched on to my mother to be nursed was perfect.

One thing that wasn't perfect during my coming into this world was that my mother had a tear while pushing me out, which led her to need stitches. That non perfect moment, however, was turned into something perfect. The doctor said to my mother, "You really have a special one you brought into the world; your stitches are in the shape of a star." You couldn't make this up! I was home with my parents in less than two days because of how quickly I was born, and they said this room could be used for a mother who truly needed it.

At every doctor's appointment, there were tests to see where I was and if I was meeting my milestones. I smiled when they smiled and laughed when they made silly faces. I had so much personality. Even in the office visits, they still referred to me as the "perfect baby." I barely cried when I got shots—well, at least not until I got home and realized what had happened to me.

I learned everything right on time. At three months, I was grasping for things, following objects and trying to sit up. Rolling around? I had that down pat. By six months, I was crawling and ready to take on the world with my friends in Gymboree. At nine months, I was standing while holding onto the couch and scaling all the furniture that was close enough for me to reach. And at twelve months, I spoke my first word! "Dada." "Pongebob." "Doggy." Words came easily, like tiny songs dancing on my tongue. I pointed, I called out, I named the world around me. And when music played, I sang along in my own way, humming and clapping to the rhythm—especially singing to my favorite show, *SpongeBob SquarePants*. I would sing the theme song so loud and proud that eventually, everyone in my home learned the words and joined in.

My mom would say prayers with me every night and I would conclude the prayers by saying "Amen." My world was full of sound, and I was a part of it. Everything seemed so normal. I enjoyed playing with my family and having playdates. For my first birthday, I partied with the "Backyardigans" and even though I was not walking yet, it was still a great celebration. I was talking and communicating with everyone around me. My "Hi's" to family, friends, and even strangers were vibrant. My eye contact and hugs were deep and intentional. I enjoyed being around people. Even at that age, energy was important, and I was able to feel people's energy. The majority of my world felt like good vibes, which kept me laughing and happy.

And then, at fifteen months, the words disappeared. The world that I knew and loved shifted. I don't know where it went. One day, it was there, and the next, it was gone. I opened my mouth, but nothing came out. The sounds were still inside me, spinning and swirling, but they wouldn't escape. People waited for me to speak, their faces expectant, hopeful. But I couldn't. The music had stopped, and I didn't know how to bring it back.

The light in my mother's eye started to dim. She seemed to be scared even though the hugs, kisses and prayers continued. But now there seemed to be a fear beneath it all. Because I had always been so attuned to the energy around me, my sensitivity was heightened to the tenth power. The look in their eyes, the tears I noticed—that I had never seen before—started to make me question and worry about what was happening around me.

The changes I felt from the grown-ups made me feel anxious, and I began to question how they now felt about me. The hugs felt different—almost as if they felt sorry for me. My mother and I had prayed every night and usually our prayers were about protection, our family, and thanking

God for our blessings. They felt so cheerful and full of hope. After I stopped talking, we continued to pray but they felt different. They sounded desperate, sad and hopeless. Even though she still prayed for protection and expressed gratitude, it no longer sounded cheerful.

Once the big people around me started to change, so did I. I stopped engaging with others and no longer gave eye contact to any of them. It was almost like I couldn't; they were changing in front of me so quickly. I wasn't upset, I just couldn't understand what was happening. Inside, I still felt like the same Cameron. I just wasn't talking to them in the same way. But since they started to look at me like a different kid, I shut down! I no longer responded to my name, and I would hear them say things like, "She's really focused on her tablet" or "She really is locked into her show." The truth was, I could hear them, but until you were willing to truly see me, I didn't want to respond.

The world that once clapped for my every new word now waited in silence, unsure of what to do with me. My world was changing quickly. Now, we are meeting with all these different physicians. Even though these doctors were very smart and specialized in childhood development, they looked just as worried as my family did. Every now and then, I would have a doctor who entered the same way my office visits used to go when I was meeting all my milestones. There were some who still treated me like I had a voice. They laughed with me and talked to me, even though they were laying serious information on my parents. Those appointments reminded me that there are some people in this world that will not see my label before they truly see me.

We went through that process for nine months. It was doctor after doctor. They didn't want to put a label on me without exploring all the options. They wanted to see what it was like for me being around more children consistently, explore speech therapy and just give it time—to see if the words would come back. They didn't. And finally at 24 months they diagnosed me with Autism. Now that there was a label, the looks intensified, the fear grew , and the discomfort seemed to heighten. By this point, I had already adjusted to looks and stares. I was doing things differently too— picking up objects and smelling them, putting things in my mouth that I wouldn't usually do, peeling tape off of objects and sticking it to my face because the sensation felt so calming.

Oh, and I had to have some type of fidget in my hand— it truly grounded me. It was also a way for me to silence the world because it was so loud. Jumping up and down, creating my own unique sounds became my new language. They weren't your usual sounds, and many people stared and rolled their eyes when we were in places meant to be quiet. My mother never stopped taking me to places we usually went to like Disney on Ice, the library, circus, restaurants and vacations on a plane. The world made me feel like I didn't belong there, but the music in my head continued to tell me to keep dancing to my own rhythm.

As much as I was internally happy and still felt the love from my loved ones, they still seemed confused—unsure how to interact with me. Once I stopped speaking, there would be times when people would walk into our home and no longer say hello to me.

My mother loved on me so much, but I could see the question in her eyes: *Where was her "perfect" baby?* Life had changed for me—drastically—in just the first two years of my life.

"With You" - Chris Brown

Chapter 2:
The World Moves Without Me

The world didn't slow down when my words disappeared. People still spoke to me, but now their voices carried something different—hesitation, uncertainty, even pity. I could feel it in their tones, in the way their eyes searched mine, waiting for something I could no longer give. Even though I was trying to adjust to the changes, I really couldn't. It went from people calling me the "perfect baby," stopping my mother just to touch my hair, or comment on my looks and how I dressed—to treating me like I was invisible. Everything that was happening inside of me, I was able to manage because it felt like I still had control within myself. But the way the world started to look at me—that was the hardest part.

At home, the changes were subtle but sharp. My mother still smiled, still kissed my forehead, still wrapped me in her arms. But I could feel the questions behind her eyes, the quiet worry in her prayers. She held me tighter, as if trying to squeeze the words out of me. I could even sense her frustration when she would try to get me to say something and all I gave was a silent smile.

As much as I knew my mother would do anything for me, I started to see her the way I had begun to see the rest of the world—unsafe. Not because she didn't love me, but because she didn't understand. And I know it wasn't her fault. Even though she was a therapist, she couldn't make sense of what was happening with her "perfect" baby. I could see the blame she placed on herself—thinking she did something to cause this. Even though her hugs felt filled with worry, I tried to hug her tighter—to reassure her that I was still okay.

Outside, the world moved as if I wasn't there. Strangers who once greeted me with bright "Hellos!" now spoke over me, not to me. At family gatherings, conversations skipped past me like I wasn't even present. The world was learning to live without my voice, but I was still here. I have always been here. Even if they no longer heard me, I was still speaking—in the ways I knew how.

I found comfort in rhythm—the tapping of my fingers against my leg, the rocking of my body to a silent beat. Music still made sense, even when the words didn't. I hummed when the world was too loud. I clapped when my feelings grew too big to hold inside. I listened—really listened—to the way the world moved, and I answered in ways only I could understand. The way I connected to the world was different. It had always been different, but now that I don't speak, it really was noticeable. I hear everything at a different level. Things taste different. I don't like certain textures. Some textures make me feel uncomfortable while others make me feel calm. I don't know which textures will do what until I try them all.

I love music. However, some songs—depending on the pitch and instruments—can make me really excited and some can make me cover my ears. I'm learning all these things about myself while also navigating how people are responding to me.

Then came school—a place where words were everything. A place where silence was a problem to be solved. Regular school wasn't a good fit for me. That's where I started to understand the cold things people were saying about me. They were saying things that were true, but I guess it was the way they said them. I wasn't doing the things typical kids were doing, like tying their shoes, reading and writing. I was academically and socially behind my typical peers. But I was still me. Still a person with a very big purpose in this world.

I remember a time when my parents were observing me in a classroom with typical peers. After the observation period, the teacher looked at me, then turned to my parents and said, "She doesn't belong here."

I felt her words.

That was the beginning of me questioning that very thing in various settings. There are quite a few places that are not a good fit for me—and I know that. However, I don't want people to assume that's true for *every* place.

I am here!

I was so excited to go to a school with other people who had disabilities. Maybe I would feel like I belong there. There were so many bright lights and a lot of noise, but I was happy to be around other people who were like me. Even though we shared similar diagnoses, we were all still different in our own ways—but I felt like they understood me more than the outside world did.

As a girl, not many of my peers looked like me. There was only one other girl in my class—her name was Monay, but the teachers called her "MoMo." It felt so good to have another girl in my class. Even though she was non-verbal, we had a special 'look', we would dart to one another when funny things happened in class or when one of us felt uncomfortable. There was a sense of safety I felt with MoMo—and we had that girl power. I was so blessed to share a classroom with MoMo for six years. We got to see each other grow in ways that people thought we wouldn't and we also experienced each other's regressions. No matter what happened, we always maintained 'that look' between us. MoMo and I never sat next to each other, but we responded to one another wherever we were in the room.

There was one time in class MoMo got upset because someone touched her arm—she didn't like to be touched, especially on her arms. She started screaming and I remembered one of her favorite fidgets. I walked across the room, handed it to her, and went back to my seat. When I looked back at her there it was—that glance we gave one another—and she had calmed down. We didn't speak to each other besides the looks, but we held one another down for all those years. We understood each other, even while surrounded by all boys. Without words, MoMo and I seemed to get it. I couldn't understand why the rest of the world couldn't pay attention to my eyes and vocalizations in the same way she did.

The teachers really tried. I didn't see the same type of worry in their eyes. However, when I was frustrated and couldn't express myself, I could see the confusion—and sometimes what looked like defeat—in them. In my mind, I just wanted to encourage them to not give up. I just needed to get these emotions out before I exploded. Just give me a few more minutes, and I will feel regulated. Many of the teachers started to *learn* me well enough to understand my patterns and the kinds of things that made me feel dysregulated. The more I noticed the feelings the big people in my life had about what I was experiencing, the more it made me not want to soothe myself by making noises, jumping up and down, or rocking. I couldn't tell if I was too much for them to handle. I was trying to understand what they were thinking and feeling as well as trying to control what I was thinking and feeling. It made my days feel so emotionally heavy. I wanted people to connect with me, rather than trying to figure me out like I was some kind of problem to be solved. Even though the world was moving on without me, I was making my way—letting them know I'm here and trying to understand this is a transition for us all.

"Superstar" - Usher

Chapter 3:
Invisible Walls

There were walls everywhere, though no one else seemed to see them. They weren't made of bricks or stone; they were made of stares, whispers, and the space people put between me and them. I felt them long before I understood what they were. I could be standing right next to someone, but it was as if I was standing on the other side of something they didn't want to cross.

The playgrounds were the first place I noticed it. When I was little, other kids ran past me, their laughter trailing like music in the air. I wanted to join them, but every time I moved closer, they shifted away. Sometimes they watched me, curious, but mostly, they ignored me. The swings creaked under the weight of friendships, while I stood still, holding my favorite fidget, rocking slightly.

I enjoyed things that weren't always appropriate for my age. I liked playing in the sandbox while every other 6-year-old chased one another or swung from the monkey bars. Even though I felt the wall between myself and others, I grew very comfortable in my own company. I laughed out loud at memories that popped into my mind. I felt the sun beaming against my face, and a gentle breeze brushing my cheeks. Nature was my friend on the playground.

I remember once standing near a group of girls who were drawing with chalk. Their colors stretched across the pavement in swirls and stars. I bent down, eager to join, holding a piece of blue chalk in my hand. Before I could press it to the ground, one of the girls whispered, "Why is she doing that?" I wasn't sure what "that" was. Maybe it was the way I rocked, or the way I hummed and made distinct noises when I was excited. It could have been putting the chalk to my nose because I enjoy connecting through smell. Whatever it was, it was enough. They moved their drawings further away. I kept drawing with my chalk, and even though my design didn't look like theirs, I felt like mine was a masterpiece. I enjoyed drawing on the ground, and I also realized early on that I liked the texture of the chalk against my skin. There were so many differences between me and those girls, which I was ok with—I just didn't like feeling dismissed.

Birthday parties were especially hard. When I got an invitation, my mom would light up with hope. She would dress me in my best fit, fix my hair with care, and tell me, *"You'll have so much fun!"* But I often stood at the edge of the party, holding a balloon string too tightly, watching the other kids chase each other around. I was there, but I wasn't *with* them. I would smile, but they rarely smiled back. One party I went to was a paint party, and I hadn't been there for more than five minutes before an adult yelled at me for putting my fingers in the paint and putting it to my nose.

My mother had just taken off my little brother's and my coats when she saw the paint instructor grab my arm and yell at me. I saw my mother walking very fast to confront the woman. Honestly, I was more scared about what might happen to *her* because my mom doesn't play when it comes to me.

Even though my mother was still trying to navigate her feelings about the many changes I was going through, she was very protective of me. She had no problem checking someone who mistreated me. She would handle them in the most educational yet aggressive manner. It was funny because she was trying to teach them about autism but also letting them know not to play with her daughter. Thankfully, someone my mother knew intervened before it escalated. Times like that, I wanted to talk so badly—to tell my mother even though she is protecting me, I didn't like seeing her upset. When she yelled at people, it made me scared.

We made it through that party, and for the most part, I knew my mother hadn't really shaken it off. Many of the activities were not appropriate for me, so I just enjoyed being by myself—literally moving to my own beat in my head. I will never forget the ride home from that party. My mother promised me, *"It doesn't matter whose birthday it is—I will no longer put you in predicaments that make you feel uncomfortable or in things that I know you are not interested in."* She has kept her word since then.

Sometimes the adults made it worse. I heard the gentle, pitying tones when they spoke to my mother. *"She's so sweet"* or *"It must be hard,"* they would say, their eyes flicking to me before quickly looking away. They thought I didn't understand, but I did. They saw me as work, as a burden. I was not the child to invite to playdates; I was an exception, a challenge. Invites became fewer and farther between. I was becoming comfortable with not attending events because I felt disconnected from most of those people anyway. I did enjoy going to Disney on Ice, the Ringling Brothers Circus and the movies. Most of those places are filled with laughter, screams and cries—so my high-pitched yells, and sporadic laughs fit right in. The looks I received at those places didn't last too long because most people were tuned in to the show.

The walls were everywhere—at the park, at school, at the grocery store. When my mom tried to include me in conversations, people would nod politely but direct their words back to her, as if I wasn't there. I wanted to scream, *I am here!*—but my voice was not one they were willing to hear.

The walls made me feel small, but they also made me strong. In those quiet moments, I found other ways to be seen. MoMo still looked at me the way she always did. We didn't need words. The music I hummed grew louder in my heart. And when my mother looked at me—sometimes past her worry—I could still see her love shining through.

I hoped that one day, someone would climb over those walls to reach me. Until then, I would keep singing my silent song, hoping that someone, somewhere, would finally listen.

"Roar"- Katy Perry

Chapter 4:
A New Chapter In My Body

Change has never asked for my permission. It simply arrives—sudden, unavoidable—shifting the ground beneath me. But this change was different. It was not in the world around me; it was within me.

One day, there was nothing. The next, there was blood.

I didn't understand it at first. My body, which had always been my safe place—my place of rhythm and comfort—suddenly felt like a stranger. The sensations were new, uncomfortable: wetness, warmth, and pain that hummed low in my belly like a distant drum. I wanted to ask what was happening. I wanted to tell someone that I was scared. But the words, as always, stayed locked inside.

So, I watched. I listened. I felt the shift in my mother's energy when she noticed—her gentle hands, her soft voice telling me it was okay. That this was normal. That I was growing up. But I wasn't sure I wanted to grow up—especially if it meant *this*. She asked me to use my device to describe how I felt about now having a period. I couldn't even find the words on my device. Sometimes I wouldn't answer her. Other times, I would say what I would always say to get her to stop asking: "happy." The truth was I really didn't know what I was feeling besides confusion. I felt so many things at once and that was a little scary. It felt like a flood of emotions all at once, and I couldn't control them. Even the things I usually used to soothe myself weren't effective during my cycle. I couldn't figure out what worked, it made everyone around me just as confused about what to do.

This was a new chapter of being different. A new challenge. And once again, I would have to find my own way to speak through the silence.

Months before my menstruation actually started, I knew something was happening to my body, but I couldn't make sense of it. There had been so many changes on and off throughout the twelve years of my life. I thought this was one of those autistic-type changes but no—this actually was one of those *normal* types of changes. I became very agitated and aggressive every month before my period started. I was usually very happy and cuddly. During the week before my period, I would bite my arm, and push teachers out of my personal space. At home, I wanted to be alone in my room. At times, I would even be aggressive toward my parents and siblings. I felt bad about my behavior, but it was also something I couldn't control. It was like this rage that was inside of me that needed to come out. My teachers and doctors told my mother that my menstrual cycle may be starting soon: however, seven months went by and nothing came. Finally, one month it started—and every month thereafter. But, when it was over, I was back to my happy, cuddly self. I could feel when that time of the month was coming but I couldn't figure out how to tell the grownups in my life. I wanted not only to prepare myself, but also to prepare them.

My school did a great job of creating a social story that they shared with my parents. We read the social story at home, and over time, I became more comfortable with understanding what was happening with my body. I even started to express my true feelings on my device about how I felt during that time. I began to identify things that were effective for me, such as alone time, longer showers, listening to music louder than usual, and extra snacks. Based on my mother's description of herself during her cycle, I actually felt like I was one of the girls. What I was going through was similar to others even if mine was more dramatic at times.

There were times I wished MoMo and I were still in the same class—just to give each other that comforting look. Having another girl with autism, who also had a period, meant we would have truly understood each other. But that wasn't the case, I'm now in middle school, in a class with all boys. I didn't realize how meaningful it was to have another girl with autism around daily until I didn't have it anymore. MoMo and I went to different middle schools, and it didn't really hit me until I *needed* her presence. Even though we were non-verbal, we just always got it!

Even though I have been trying to adjust to this new change, there were some things that were uncomfortable, and I had no words to express this to my loved ones. So, I would always just have a blank stare whenever my period came, almost trying to cue the big people with my eyes, gazing down to my pants. I didn't like the feeling of the sanitary napkin in my underwear. It was such a sensory discomfort. I was not used to having to wear something on me for several days. I had to learn how to let the adults know when I wanted to change my pad. Until then, there were many times I was ignored because it didn't *look* like it needed to be changed. After close observation, it eventually caught their attention that I didn't like the feeling. I changed sanitary napkins quite frequently—every hour I believe. I truly felt seen. I was able to communicate my needs during such a challenging time.

I really felt bad for my dad. He just didn't know what to do when I was at his home. He would call my mom and ask to change weekends when my cycle started. My mother would tell him he had to work through it—and he did. We did a lot of learning together. He seemed so scared for me. I wanted to learn my new system not only to support myself but also to give my dad some relief. The more I adjusted to having my period, the more he grew in understanding this new development in my world. He learned to give me my space, kept extra snacks during that time, and let me blast Chris Brown on the way home from school. Each month that has gone by, I feel more and more confident in handling my body. I'm so proud of myself and my village because we triumphed in this transition well. We all adjusted and made accommodations to support me as best as possible. There were many times I felt invisible growing up—however, every month, having my menstrual cycle gave me a voice that they couldn't ignore!

"Stronger" - Kelly Clarkson

Chapter 5: Understanding Me

I have always known I was different. Long before I heard the word *autism*, and before I understood that my silence set me apart, I could feel it. It was in the way people looked at me, the way they spoke around me instead of to me. It was in the way my body moved when I was excited, the way sounds felt louder, colors looked brighter, and touches lingered longer than they seemed to for others. Once the label of autism was given, it seemed it gave people around me some relief. However, it didn't really mean anything to me. All it really did was make me feel like I was walking around with a sign on my shirt that read "It's OK—she's jumping and making distinct noises because she has Autism." And the world would respond back, "Oh, OK, we kind of get it." Having a diagnosis didn't really do anything for me. I realized adults needed a label to make sense out of everything. I don't care about that kind of stuff. I care about trying to normalize my experiences and being treated fairly.

But *knowing* I was different and understanding *why*, were two very different things.

As I got older, I started noticing more things. I noticed the way other girls whispered and giggled together, as they shared secrets with words that flowed so easily. I noticed how teachers spoke slower when they talked to me—their smiles a little too wide, their voices a little too careful. The people who would talk louder like I couldn't hear always made my mother laugh. My mom would just say to people "Why are you speaking so loud? She can hear you!" I noticed how people expected me to fit into a world that wasn't made for me. At a young age, I had to figure out how I would create my own safe space for myself and not expect the outside world to do it for me.

For a long time, I wondered: *Who am I supposed to be? Am I just the quiet girl? The girl who stims? The girl who needs help? Or am I more?* As much as I knew how different I was, I also knew I was so special and unique. I knew I was so much more. I knew that when I hugged people, I had a gift that could transform their day. I learned that my smile and laughter are contagious. I learned to quiet the voices that said I was too loud, or that my laughter was obnoxious. I learned that I taught my loved ones how to be present in each moment. I knew the way I connected with Mother Nature was such a gift—the way water soothed me and seemed to enjoy my presence. I knew I was more than just a little girl who couldn't talk; I was a girl who was brought here to teach others how to listen in such a profound way, with no words. I knew I had to teach people that labels don't define the essence of who you are. Wearing designer clothes and how you dress doesn't really matter to me. What matters is being connected with yourself and loved ones— is happiness. That is what success is. I am so happy that I learned I was so much more than a label. I have a diagnosis of autism, but it is not my entire being. At such a young age I feel I have a sound understanding of who I am—more than some adults. We are concerned and connected about different things. I don't care about what most typically developed people care about, I care about deep connections, not superficial things.

I didn't have the words to ask these questions out loud, but I felt them deep inside me. Little by little, I'm starting to find my own answers. Navigating these teen years has been somewhat confusing. On the one hand, I'm learning and accepting aspects of myself that seem abnormal to others. I'm more comfortable with the stares and the misunderstandings. I laugh hard and dance along to my music like no one is watching. All those things feel so freeing for me. On the other hand, it can feel lonely. I'm seventeen years old and I don't have any best friends my age. I'm not invited to go hang out at the mall. I don't have my driver's license and I'm not sneaking boys over when my parents are not home. Trust me, I'm sure many of these experiences have made my parents very happy that I'm not doing those things. But, there is a part of me that has felt like I'm missing out. I have a close relationship with my family. I watch movies with them, we travel, they listen to all the music I love. We dance and celebrate all milestones in my life. My youngest brother thinks he's older than me. He is very protective of me, and I'm appreciative of that. My mother has raised him to be my voice when people around me don't understand what I'm requesting or expressing. He also knows how protective I am over him. If my mother yells at him, I stand up so she can know I don't like it when he is in trouble. I have siblings with whom I have learned how to play games and share with over the years. I have a sister who is also protective of me. She is now twenty years old, and of course, our lives look completely different. She was one of my first friends outside of MoMo.

I feel like I have more control over my life and understanding who I am since I became more comfortable with my talking device. I have tried so many different methods to communicate over the years. Some were too advanced for me, other devices may have been too small for my fingers and the rest I outgrew. One year, a speech and language therapist offered me a program designed to grow with me—even into adulthood, with buttons for each stage of my life. With this new program, I am able to use complete sentences. There are pictures of my family members, pictures of me doing tasks in my home—it covers everything I deal with. I feel empowered when I have my device. There are times I feel seen when I'm pressing my buttons several times in a person's face because they have no choice but to listen to me. Even though it's not my voice, it works just as well. When my device dies and needs to be charged, I use my other modes of communicating; however, I look forward to it being charged so I can get the attention that I need.

There are other events that I feel like I am missing out on, like proms, senior trips, and college tours. However, the truth is, I probably wouldn't care about many of those things anyway. The world makes it seem like it is a requirement to do those things at a certain age. If you don't do those things, then something must be wrong with you. These are not the things that I am doing in my teen years, but people don't know what to ask me about if it doesn't look like those typical things. That is the part that feels lonely at times. Truly, I don't have a desire for those things; however, I do have a desire for connection and people being interested in me even if it doesn't fit the norm.

Understanding me has been fun, scary, interesting and even confusing at times. I know that this journey is a forever thing of discovering me, but for right now I am extremely proud of the way I have been navigating these years. Most importantly I have been loving toward myself. I accept all aspects about myself more and more each day. I don't try to put myself in a box that others try to. Even though my parents and family had much worry and doubt about raising me with a label of autism, one thing they deposited in me is that I am enough!

"Thinking Out Loud" - Ed Shearan

Chapter 6:
Bridges and Walls

Understanding myself was one thing, but understanding how I fit into the lives of others was something completely different.

The connections I have with people are like bridges—some strong and steady, others fragile and hard to cross. There have been moments when the bridges felt wide and open, making me feel seen and loved. Other times, I could feel walls being built between me and the people around me—walls of misunderstanding, fear, or simply not knowing how to reach me. I believe many people want to have a strong bridge with me; however, by not truly understanding what autism is, they are unaware of the wall that is created.

My family has always been my strongest bridge. They hold space for me in a way that makes me feel like I belong exactly as I am. But even with them, there are moments of disconnection—times when I want to express something but can't find a way to make them understand. In my seventeen years, I have gone through several different types of communication styles. I used the Picture Exchange Communication System (PECS) for years. That was very helpful for those around me to understand because it was easy to read the pictures. However, there were times I didn't use the right picture to describe what I meant. I learned some basic sign language. My family also learned those basic signs and taught them to people around us who spent significant time with me. I also use a communication device, which has pictures on the program and speaks when I press them. I have used that communication mode for most of my life. I am able to create full sentences with my device, and I take it with me everywhere I go. Even though I have used multiple modes of communication, there are times I still don't know how to express what I am feeling—and those moments make the walls feel higher, even if they are only temporary.

Outside of my family, building bridges has been harder. Caregivers, teachers, and even other kids have tried to connect with me, but not everyone knows how. Some people stop trying if I don't respond right away, not understanding that I feel everything—even if I can't always show it. Others try too hard, making me feel like a project instead of a person. Still, there have been a few special people who have met me halfway—who saw me for who I am and not just what I couldn't do.

I attended a private school when I was two years old. I had not received an official diagnosis of autism yet; however, I had already stopped talking. My mother had explained this to both teachers in the class. With one of the teachers, there was a wall that went up pretty quickly. The other teacher, Ms. Jay immediately made a connection with me. She saw me—and I saw her. She was so genuine. She was protective of me.

There were behaviors I began to develop that the other two-year-olds weren't doing like stimming, I sought after everything that had a texture and would rub it on my face. I started playing alone. I was the only kid in the class that was potty trained, and Ms. Jay celebrated every time I went to the bathroom. She gave me such great confidence in myself. Ms. Jay advocated for me to other administrative staff when they started to say things like I didn't belong there. Ms. Jay was one of the special ones. She taught me early on that there will be some people who see me for me— with no expectations.

I had a speech therapist who was also one of those rare ones that just *got* me immediately. I enjoyed going to her sessions, even though I had already been in school all day, then spent two hours in a program for children with autism, and by 7 p.m., had a session with my girl Patty. I would be exhausted, but I knew I was going to a place where someone would be gentle with me. Patty became family, and she was my speech therapist for six years. I will never forget Patty, even though I don't see her anymore. Those connections are rare, but they remind me that even when walls go up, there are always ways to build bridges— if both sides are willing.

Feeling safe and seen is what makes those bridges strong. It's not always about what someone says or does—it's how they make me feel. Ms. Jay and Patty made me feel like I was enough just as I am. They didn't try to change me or force me to be something I couldn't be. They met me where I was, and that made all the difference. When someone takes the time to learn how I communicate, what makes me feel comfortable, and respects my space, I feel safe. Those are the moments when I can open up and let people in.

The walls don't make me feel like people don't care about me. I believe many do care about me and my well-being. But I do feel that, for some, it's not important enough to truly learn about things I'm experiencing and then go a little further to actually get to know *me*. I have had experiences where I felt the wall was up and they were not willing to lower it.

When I was eight years old, my mother was looking for a summer camp in Baltimore. Someone told her about a recreational program which was supposedly equipped to support children with special needs, especially autism. But within an hour of dropping me off, she was called and told to come pick me up because the camp "wasn't a good fit". Even though the camp was not equipped for children with special needs, their approach toward me was unloving. They yelled when I was jumping and dancing during the morning instruction. They kept telling me to stay still as we walked in a line transitioning to another area. It felt like the staff didn't even know I was coming. Many of the volunteers were teenagers working in the Summer Youth Program. This organization showed me, and my family, that they were not willing to learn about autism or embrace diversity. I was so happy to see my mother, because I didn't feel safe. As soon as I saw her, I told her on my device: "Finish" and "All done." She knew exactly what I meant.

The walls or bridges we build are both choices. Ms. Jay and Patty made the choice to connect with me. The summer camp organization, on the other hand, made the choice to put up walls. They used false advertising to get special needs families to sign up, but they weren't willing to follow through. That was their choice too. Every choice—whether to build a bridge or put up a wall—can have a powerful effect on someone and their families. One way or another, your choice matters.

"Lean on Me" - Stevie Wonder

Chapter 7:
The Weight of Expectations

Expectations are like invisible weights that people place on you without ever asking if you're strong enough to carry them.

I know people have expectations of me. Some are spoken out loud, like when a teacher says, *"I know you can do this if you just try harder."* Others are unspoken but hang heavy in the air—expectations to behave a certain way, to learn at a certain pace, or to fit into a world that wasn't built with someone like me in mind. Those expectations don't just come from strangers or teachers—they come from people who love me, too. I know my family wants the best for me, and I can feel how proud they are of everything I accomplish. But even love can feel heavy when you know someone is hoping for something you're not sure you can give.

The expectations that are placed on me—by both loved ones and others—are not coming from a negative place. I don't believe they mean any harm. But I also don't think people fully realize how deeply those expectations impact me. Maybe it's their desire for things to *look* normal.

In my toddler years the expectations appeared to be lighter. There were other kids who weren't developing as quickly, so I was able to blend in more easily when I was under five. But as I got older, those expectations grew. I couldn't just blend in anymore. People wanted answers—why, at that age I couldn't do and act according to what they expected. Now that I'm seventeen, it feels the heaviest. Other teens my age are preparing to leave for college and start jobs. That's not what I'm doing. It was a lot easier when I was younger.

I wish people understood that I already try hard every single day. I try to communicate, even when my words won't come out. I try to stay calm, even when my body feels like it's on fire with sensations I can't control. I try *not* to dance, even though I constantly hear the rhythm vibrating through my body. I try to fit into spaces that aren't always made for me—where the noise is too loud, the lights are too bright, or the rules don't make sense. Just being in the world is hard work, even if it doesn't always look that way from the outside.

My mother used to take me to every live show since I was able to walk. She would get front row seats, and the characters would come over and greet us. It was insanely loud and crowded at those shows. Her intentions were pure, she just wanted to have those experiences with me. She expected me to enjoy it as well because I watched those characters on television. However, at a live show, it was a completely different experience for me. The older I got, the longer stares lingered, and the louder my noises became.

There were times my mother didn't realize her need to have *normal* outings superseded what *I* wanted. One year, at a live Disney play, I screamed so loud during the show, but it wasn't the usual sound I would make in those environments. She looked at me—I mean really looked at me—and she said, *"You don't want to be here, do you?"* I signed to her, *NO*.

She finally got it.

As we drove away from the arena, I watched her tears flow as I bopped to my favorite songs. When we got home, she said she was sorry, and that we wouldn't go to any more live shows again. I just smiled and hugged her. I was happy that she *finally* got it.

The hardest expectations are the ones that make me feel like who I am isn't enough. There are things people describe as basic, such as sitting still, maintaining eye contact, greeting guests and engaging with others—all of these social rules. I've learned that those things matter to other people more than they matter to me. Even down to birthdays, *every day* feels like a celebration for me. I enjoy birthdays just for the cake, not the party, gifts or people. My mother had to learn that lesson the hard way. By the time I was seven years old, I had been to Disney World five times. My birthday is in July, which is the hottest and most crowded time to go.

The last time we went, I fell on the floor in the middle of the park and refused to get up. She finally got it—I didn't need to do *this* for my birthday. Just give me the cake and some water to swim in, and that is a perfect celebration for me.

Then there are the things I want people to notice—how deeply I feel music, how I can memorize the way to a place after going there just once, and how I can sense people's moods even when they don't say a word. But those things don't always fit into what the world expects, so they go unnoticed. When I touch people for too long, they usually become uncomfortable and try to tell me to pay attention to personal space—but closeness with people is important to me. I smell people because that's the way I connect and remember them, by using my senses. I love schedules and routines; they make me feel like I have some control over my body. Many people can wing it when things change. For me, I feel completely out of sorts and then I spend a significant amount of time trying to regulate myself.

Over the years, I started to use my voice in different ways to let the adults know what I do and don't like—and also things that make me uncomfortable. Even though it may have been different from what they wanted, I started to feel more confident in expressing my wants and needs. It was my way of teaching people how to treat me. I now remind my teachers and my loved ones how important my schedule is to me and how it makes me feel safe. I feel empowered the more I express what is important to me.

My mind is always talking to me, even if my mouth doesn't. I have whole conversations in my head about the person I wish people could see. I wish they could see how smart I am, how funny I can be, how much I love to make people laugh. I laugh so much because I'm recalling things that have happened, and I want to share those memories with others. I wish they could see that just because I need help with some things, it doesn't mean I don't want independence. School reminds me that my grade level doesn't match my age level, but there are still many things I can do on my own. I want to be understood for who I am—not for what I can or can't do according to someone else's guidelines.

There are moments when I feel like I'm letting people down without ever meaning to—when I don't respond fast enough, when I don't meet a goal someone else set for me, or when I need more time to learn a task. But what if I'm not falling behind? What if I'm just on a different path altogether?

The weight of expectations is heavy, but I've learned that I don't have to carry every weight that someone hands me. Some expectations are meant to be let go—especially the ones that try to shrink me into something smaller than I was made to be. I have learned to love all aspects of myself: from my loud laughter to my short hair, the way I jump freely, the way I groove to music—both the kind that's playing and the kind in my head—the way I love and hug intensely, and the way I remember things like an elephant. I take pride in truly moving to the beat of my own band!

I know I will always have to work harder to prove myself to the world. I went to a pumpkin patch in October, and I started organizing the cakes in the store. The clerk was very annoyed and asked why I was organizing the cakes. My mother's approach to questions like that has improved over the years. She kindly informed the woman of my special needs and assured her that I was being helpful, not disruptive to anyone in the store. The woman went on to say my mom should have shared my diagnosis when we entered the store. That comment made me feel that some people's opinions of me won't be based on the person I am, but on the diagnosis I've been given. But maybe the world needs to work harder too—to see beyond its expectations and accept me for who I am.

"Can't Help but Wait" - Trey Songs

Chapter 8:
Finding Her Place

Belonging isn't just about being somewhere—it's about being seen, valued, and accepted exactly as you are.

I have spent my whole life trying to find where I fit in this world. The truth is, there aren't many spaces built with someone like me in mind. I've always felt like I'm standing on the outside looking in, waiting for someone to open the door and invite me to stay. But the longer I've lived, the more I've realized—maybe I don't need to wait for anyone to open the door. Maybe the world needs to break down the walls and build something entirely new. Just because people who are like me enjoy different things doesn't mean we don't want to feel like we are part of the community. We may just need to leave the community when it becomes overwhelming.

Belonging isn't something you can always see—it's something you feel deep inside your body. For me, belonging feels like the bass of a song that matches the rhythm of my heart. It feels like the water wrapping around me in the pool, holding me without asking me to be anything but still. It smells like my favorite lotion or the scent of someone I love—familiar, safe, and warm. Belonging is when the world makes space for me—without asking me to shrink.

There are moments when the world gets it right—like the water park with staff who spoke to me, not around me. They didn't need my mom to explain who I was or what I needed—they just treated me like I belonged there. I don't always remember their names, but I remember how they made me feel. I remember the places that made room for me without making a big deal out of it. Those places feel like home. One day I was in a tea shop with my mom, and the cashier directly asked me what I wanted to order. She gave me eye contact and was not referring to my mother. I tapped "pizza" on my device, and she gently smiled and said, "I love pizza. I wish we had that for both of us." She engaged me, I felt like I belonged.

I've learned that there's a difference between inclusion and belonging. Inclusion is when people let you sit at the table. Belonging is when they save you a seat because they know you'll be there. Inclusion is making space. Belonging is making someone feel like they were always meant to be there.

My vision of belonging isn't about changing who I am to fit into the world—it's about the world making room for people like me. I dream of stores where no one stares if I dance to the music playing overhead, or if I need to wear my headphones to block out the noise. I imagine classrooms where every child learns in their own way, without anyone being made to feel broken for needing extra time. I wish for friendships where I don't have to fight to be understood—where the way I connect is enough, just as it is.

I don't want the world to make a special place for people like me—I want the world to make every place welcoming for everyone. I don't need a movie showing once a month at 8 a.m. to feel like I belong. I want to go to the same shows at the same time as everyone else, without the stares or the whispers. I want the world to stop waiting for people like me to fit in—and start breaking down the walls that keep us out.

Nature doesn't ask the fish to fly like the birds. The sky doesn't try to quiet the wind. Every part of nature is exactly as it was made to be—and it all belongs. Maybe the world could learn something from that. Nature feels like home to me because everything has its own place, but all is connected.

Belonging doesn't have to be complicated. It's a choice—a choice to listen, to learn, and to accept. It's a choice to see people not for what they lack, but for everything they are. The world I wish for isn't perfect or free of challenges, but it's a world where every person is celebrated for who they are—not just tolerated for what they aren't. I can just envision it; it's like everyone at a dance party listening to their favorite Chris Brown and Usher songs. People fear differences so much that many are not open to realizing how many things we may actually have in common. When my mother tells people about me, their facial expressions are so funny like "Oh, she really likes pizza." I laugh at those moments. There are many things I enjoy that I watch other people engage in, we just might engage in them in different ways. But we're still at the same party. When people hear my playlist, they are so surprised that I play Ed Sheeran, Luther Vandross, Katy Perry, Usher, Chris Brown, Cardi B, Trey Songz, and so many more. If the world was more open, they would learn there is at least one thing they could connect with me on.

There are people in my life who have shown me what belonging feels like—my family, Ms. Jay, Patty, and a few others along the way. They made space for me without ever asking me to be anyone other than myself. They didn't just let me in—they built a place where I could feel safe, loved, and free. I wish the whole world could be more like them.

I'm still finding my place—and maybe I always will. But I know now that I have a place—because I exist, because I feel, because I matter. The world doesn't have to understand me completely to make room for me. It just has to be willing to try.

Dear World,

I don't need a special showtime or a quiet room to feel like I belong.

I need you to stop waiting for me to fit into your world—and start making room for me in it. Remember we are all LOVE. Let that lead you when you interact with me.

I'm already here. Will you see me?

> *"Beautiful People" - Chris Brown*

Chapter 9:
The Language of My Heart

People often think that if you can't speak, you don't have anything to say. But my heart is full of words—it just speaks a different language.

I've never needed a voice to feel deeply, to love fully, or to express what matters to me. My silence isn't empty. It's layered with thoughts, emotions, memories, and dreams. Sometimes, I wonder what it would feel like to say exactly what's on my mind the moment I feel it. But then I remember that my way of expressing myself is just as powerful, even if it takes a little more time to hear.

The world is built around spoken words, but my world is made of other things—music, touch, movement, color, rhythm, and energy. I express myself when I laugh unexpectedly at a memory that plays in my mind like a movie. I speak through the playlists I create, filled with songs that mirror my mood when I can't explain it out loud. I show love when I linger a little longer during a hug and even the way I intentionally smell people, or when I bring someone their favorite snack without being asked. My art, my actions, the way I move through the world—these are my sentences. My glances are paragraphs. My joy is poetry.

I remember once, during a family gathering, there were too many people talking at once. The room felt like it was spinning—voices layered on top of each other, chairs scraping the floor, music playing from the kitchen. I couldn't focus on any one sound, so I pulled out my iPad and typed one word: 'outside'. My mom saw it right away. She didn't ask questions or try to convince me to stay. She just nodded, grabbed a blanket, and we sat outside under the stars. We didn't talk. She didn't need me to explain. That's when I knew—she understood the language of my heart. I realized she learned my love language which is to connect with nature. I didn't need to be rushed out—I just needed to switch positions, and I eventually went back inside. I was able to communicate my needs in that moment, and sometimes that is all I need.

I've found so many ways to speak without speaking. I draw sometimes—not to impress anyone, but to show how I see the world. I once drew a picture of a bunch of circles with several different colors and it didn't look like any particular design, it was more abstract. My mom looked at it for a long time and wasn't quite sure what to make of it and then she asked me. I said "happy" on my device. After that moment, when I draw colorful circles, she now asks me if I'm happy, and we can have a conversation about my feelings in that moment. When I am able to converse with my family, not only do I feel connected and seen—I can tell it makes them happy too, feeling that same connection.

I dance when I can't contain my emotions. Music enters me like lightning, and I have to let it out. My body knows how to say what my mouth can't. There's a rhythm inside me that no one taught me, but it speaks louder than words ever could. Music makes me so happy. It's like the songwriters know me personally, because they are singing what I feel. The vibration of music gives me permission to be free. No one has taught me how to create a playlist on my phone, yet I have created such a diverse one that touches on every emotion I have experienced. This is one of the easiest ways for me to communicate with my family because they all love music. When I start dancing, someone always joins me—and that is how we have a conversation. When I play Christmas songs and old school songs by Stevie Wonder, my grandmother and I dance like we are at our own party. When I play trap music, my siblings first ask, 'Cam, how do you know that song?'—and before you know it, we are communicating through movement and laughter. When I dance, it's not a performance—it's a translation of my feelings. Even when people stare or don't understand, I keep dancing—because it's mine. It's real. It's me.

There have been people—like Ms. Jay and Patty—who never needed me to say a single word to know what I was feeling. They noticed the way I looked around when I was curious, the way I rocked when I was overwhelmed, the way my whole face lit up when someone played the right song. They saw the tiny shifts that most people miss. They didn't rush me. They didn't assume. They just waited and watched with open hearts. That's what true understanding looks like.

I love food. It's another way I communicate with people. I love the texture, the taste and the preparation. I enjoy trying new foods and sharing them with my family to see if they have the same thoughts about it. I communicate by preparing food with my loved ones. I feel like I am a part of things when I am in the kitchen. I am the sous chef in both of my homes. I pass all the seasonings, wash the items being prepared, gather the cookware, and set the tone with some music. I am having a full *conversation* with my family when I am preparing a meal with them. When we have guests and they're cooking on the grill, my mother makes it known that I'm the sous chef and invites me into the preparation, which allows me to make a new connection with them. People connect over food all the time, all around the world.

These words come from deep inside me, and I know they matter—even if I'm the only one who hears them.

Sometimes I think about the things people miss when they only listen with their ears. They don't see how I gently trace the edge of a leaf when I'm thinking. They don't feel the way my body tenses when a room feels too loud. They don't know that when I smell someone's shirt or hair, it's because I'm trying to remember them in my own way. All of these things are my language. The problem isn't that I can't communicate—the problem is that not enough people are fluent in my language.

The people who take the time to learn me—those are the ones who hear me the loudest.

"Speak to My Heart" - Donnie McClurkin

Epilogue: The Voice Within

Some people think a voice is only something you can hear with your ears. But I've learned that a voice is something you feel—it's in your actions, your rhythm, your passions, and your truth. It's the way you show the world who you are, even when words don't come easily. This book, this journey, has been my way of sharing my voice—not the one made of sound, but the one made of soul.

As I look toward the future, I carry all the lessons I've lived, all the love I've been given, and all the dreams still unfolding inside me. I don't know exactly what tomorrow will look like—but I do know I'll meet it with courage, music, and the quiet power of being fully, unapologetically me.

This is my message for you—whoever you are, wherever you are: differences are not things to be feared or fixed. They are gifts to be honored. They are songs waiting to be heard. And when we take the time to truly see each other—not just for what we do, but for who we are—we all grow a little closer to the world we're meant to create.

I hope that when people read my story, they don't feel sorry for me. I hope they feel curious. I hope they feel inspired to listen differently, to see more deeply, and to treat every person like their presence matters—because it does. I hope they remember that communication doesn't always come in sentences. Sometimes it's in a smile, a dance, a drawing, or a favorite song played on repeat. Sometimes it's in the silence, too.

I'm still learning how to live in a world that doesn't always understand me. But I've also learned how to hold space for myself—to honor my needs, to find joy in my own way, and to keep showing up as I am. My voice may be different, but it's strong. And it deserves to be heard. In just seventeen years, I have learned that I am love and light—and it is my hope that you learn that about yourself as well!

So here I am, at the end of this book—but not the end of my story. My life is a song still being written, with notes of love, strength, struggle, and hope. And even if the world doesn't always get the melody, I'll keep singing it—loud, soft, in movement or stillness—because it is mine.

To anyone out there who feels different, unheard, or unseen: your voice matters. Your story matters. *You* matter.

And to everyone else—thank you for listening.

"Don't Stop the Music" - Rhianna

Final Author's Note

This book was written from the voice the world doesn't always hear—but one that has always been speaking.

As her mother, and as someone who has watched her grow into herself with grace, courage, and quiet strength, I wanted to give life to her perspective in a way that felt honest, sacred, and powerful. These words are not just my imagination—they are born from years of observation, connection, trial and error, and deep love. They are her rhythms, her truths, her unspoken songs finally allowed to sing.

To every parent walking alongside a child whose voice doesn't come easily: keep listening. Keep learning. Keep showing up. The connection you're building—even in silence—is more profound than you may realize.

To educators, therapists, neighbors, and strangers—your open mind and compassionate heart can shape someone's entire world. Inclusion is not an event—it's a commitment. One small gesture of empathy can make someone feel like they belong.

And to anyone who has ever felt different or unseen: you are not alone. Your story matters. Your presence matters. The world may not always understand you right away—but that doesn't mean you have to change who you are to be worthy of love.

Thank you for reading her story. Thank you for listening to her.

Let's continue to build a world where silence is not mistaken for emptiness, but understood as another way to sing.

With love and deep gratitude,
Sophia Cox

Acknowledgements

This book would not exist without the love, support, and unwavering belief of many incredible people.

To my daughter, Cameron Coleman—thank you for inspiring this story with your strength, your silence, and your song. You are the heartbeat of these pages, and it is your light that guides every word. Thank you for teaching me what it means to listen beyond words.

To my husband, Zavadyah Sr., and our blended family (Zy'Anna, Tyler, Ziaire, and Zavadyah Jr.)—thank you for your patience, your laughter, and the sacred space you hold for our family every day. You make room for love to lead, always.

To Alex, my partner in co-parenting, thank you for always showing up for your daughter and learning how to be tagged in when we are in the ring.

To my mother, Gale Nash, you have loved and protected Cameron since the day she was born. We truly thank you for all of your sacrifices.

To the Godparents, Sekyere and Shamikka, thank you for showing up for Cameron and having the willingness to support her in many ways.

To my starting five (Nafeesa, Shamikka, Venice, Tahira, and LaShaunna), thank you for holding space for me over these 17 years and allowing me to vent, creating a safe space for me and my family.

To Keisa, thank you for being my accountability partner as we continue to push each other and not let our Capricorn brains keep chasing perfection.

To Ms. Jay, Pat, and every educator, therapist, and support person who saw my daughter and not just her diagnosis—thank you for being part of her village and for reminding the world that inclusion begins with understanding.

To the faculty of Inner Visions Institute for Spiritual Development, I thank you for helping me to learn how to hear Cameron on a deeper level and to truly accept our journey.

To my friends and family who allow Cameron to be herself in your presence, even if she has smelled you and requested hugs and kisses 100 times—thank you for accepting her.

And most importantly, to every parent, caregiver, or soul reading this book—thank you for showing up. Thank you for listening. May this story echo in your heart and help build a world that hears every silent song.

With deepest gratitude,
Sophia Cox

About the Author

Sophia Cox is a native New Yorker from Brooklyn now residing in Maryland, where she serves as a Licensed Clinical Professional Counselor and Certified Spiritual Life Coach. She is the founder of Visions From Above, LLC—a coaching and therapeutic practice dedicated to empowering individuals and families through healing, truth, and self-discovery.

She earned her degrees from the national treasure Morgan State University and Towson University and studied under Iyanla Vanzant and the faculty of the Inner Visions Institute for Spiritual Development. She continues to support others in finding their authentic voice and remembering the truth of who they are.

Beyond her professional roles, Sophia takes the greatest pride in being Vice President of her "Party of 7"—her loving blended family of five children and her devoted husband. *Her Silent Song* is not only her debut book, but also a labor of love and a tribute to her daughter, Cameron, whose silent strength inspired every word.

Reflections

1. Describe a time when you felt invisible or unheard. What emotions came up for you, and how did you navigate that experience?

2. What does true belonging look like for you?

3. In what ways have you extended compassion—or unintentionally withheld it pertaining to people who are different from you?

4. What specific actions, conversations, or commitments can you make moving forward to increase your awareness of the autism community?

5. What is one message from this book that you want to carry with you—and share with others?

www.ingramcontent.com/pod-product-compliance
Lightning Source LLC
Chambersburg PA
CBHW030224170426
43194CB00007BA/856